The ... nifesto

In Pla...

BookCaps™ Study Guides

www.bookcaps.com

Table of Contents

About BookCaps

To see other books in the "Plain and Simple English" series, visit **www.BookCaps.com**.

Modern Version

Introduction

An invisible demon is haunting Europe -- the demon of Communism. All the Powers of old Europe have formed an alliance to chase out this demon: Pope and Czar, Metternich and Guizot, French Radicals and German police-spies.

Where is the underdog political party that has not been labeled Communistic by its rivals in power? Where the Opposition that has not thrown back the name-calling of Communism, against its own competitors?

Two things happen as a result.

I. Communism is already treated and realized by all European Powers as itself a Power.

II. It is time that Communists should openly, in front of the whole world, publish their views, their aims, their tendencies, and meet this fairytale of the Demon of Communism with a Manifesto (a statement of beliefs and goals) of the party itself.

To this end, Communists of various nationalities have assembled in London, and made a draft of the following Manifesto, to be published in the English, French, German, Italian, Flemish and Danish languages.

I cant understand you. Go Back to ure country

white power :)

5

whithe
I can't understand fyrer
rov. Go Back to the coally

I. Bourgeois and Proletarians

The history of societies up until now is the history of struggles between social classes.

Free man and slave, patrician and plebeian, lord and serf, guild-master and journeyman, in a word: oppressor and oppressed, stood in constant fighting against each another, carried on an uninterrupted, sometimes hidden, sometimes open fight - a fight that each time ended either in a revolutionary reorganization of society in general, or in everyone losing.

In the earlier periods of history, we find almost everywhere a complicated arrangement of society into several sections, all sorts of divisions in wealth and power. In ancient Rome we have patricians, knights, plebeians, slaves; in the Middle Ages, feudal lords, vassals, guild-masters, journeymen, apprentices, serfs; in almost all of these classes, again, even more specific categories.

The modern bourgeois society that has grown out of the ruins of feudal society has not gotten rid of class rivalry. It has simply established new classes, new conditions of oppression, new forms of struggle in place of the old ones. Our time period, the epoch of the bourgeoisie, has, however, this distinctive feature: it has simplified the class enemies. Society as a whole is more and more splitting up into two huge hostile camps, into two great classes, directly facing each other: Bourgeoisie and Proletariat.

From the peasants of the Middle Ages came the contract workers of the earliest towns. From these towns the first elements of the bourgeoisie were developed.

The discovery of America and the first sailing around the Cape opened up fresh ground for the rising bourgeoisie. The East-Indian and Chinese markets, the colonization of America, trade with the colonies, the increase in the ways to go about exchanging goods and services, and in goods in general, gave to commerce, to navigation, to industry, an impulse never before known, and thereby, to the revolutionary element in the tottering feudal society, a rapid development.

The medieval system of industry, under which industrial production was monopolized by closed guilds, now no longer sufficed for the growing wants of the new markets. The manufacturing system took its place. The guild-masters were pushed on one side by the manufacturing middle class; division of labour between the different corporate guilds vanished when faced with division of labour in each single workshop.

Meanwhile the markets kept growing, the demand always rising. Even the assembly line was no longer enough. As a result, steam and machinery revolutionized industrial production. The place of manufacture was taken by the giant, Modern Industry, the place of the industrial middle class, by industrial millionaires, the leaders of whole industrial armies, the modern bourgeois.

Modern industry has established the world market, for which the discovery of America made possilbe. This market has given a huge development to trade, to navigation, to communication by land. This development has, in its time, depended on industry expanding; and has grown in proportion as industry, commerce, navigation, railways extended - in the same proportion the bourgeoisie developed, increased its resources, and pushed into the background every social class handed down from the Middle Ages.

We see, therefore, how the modern bourgeoisie is itself the product of a long history of development, of a series of revolutions in the methods of production and of exchange.

Each step in the development of the bourgeoisie was accompanied by a connected political advance of that class. An oppressed class under the rule of the medieval nobility, an armed and self-governing group in the medieval town; here independent urban republic (as in Italy and Germany), there taxable "third estate" of the monarchy (as in France), afterwards, in the actual period of manufacture, serving either the semi-feudal or the absolute monarchy as a balance against the nobility, and, in fact an essential part of the great monarchies in general, the bourgeoisie has at last, since the establishment of Modern Industry and of the world-market, conquered for itself, in the modern representative State, exclusive political control. The executive branch of the modern State is simply a committee for managing the shared business of the whole bourgeoisie.

The bourgeoisie, historically, has played a very revolutionary part.

The bourgeoisie, wherever it has gotten the advantage, has put an end to all feudal, patriarchal, idyllic relations. It has without mercy torn apart the various feudal ties that connected man to his "natural superiors," and has left remaining no other connection between man and man than basic self-interest, than callous "cash payment." It has drowned the most heavenly joys of religious enthusiasm, of chivalry, of sentiment, in the icy water of self-interested calculation. It has turned personal worth into exchange value. And in place of the numberless and doable freedoms that were once considered sacred, has set up that single, impossible freedom -- Free Trade. In one word, for exploitation (taking advantage unfairly), poorly hidden by religious and political illusions: naked, shameless, direct, brutal exploitation.

The bourgeoisie has stripped of its halo every occupation once honored and looked up to with reverent respect. It has turned the doctor, the lawyer, the priest, the poet, the man of science, into its paid wage laborers.

The bourgeoisie has torn away from the family its emotional layer, and has reduced the family relation to just a money relation.

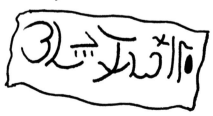

The bourgeoisie has revealed how it happened that the brutal display of energy in the Middle Ages, which Reactionists admire so much, found its suitable partner in the worst laziness. It has been the first to show what man's activity can make happen. It has accomplished wonders even more amazing than Egyptian pyramids, Roman aqueducts, and Gothic cathedrals; it has sent out expeditions that are even more impressive than all former exoduses of nations and crusades.

The bourgeoisie cannot exist without constantly revolutionizing the tools of production, and therefore the processes of production, and with them the whole processes of society. Preserving the old method of production in unaltered form, was, instead, the first condition of existence for all earlier industrial classes. Constant revolutionizing of production, uninterrupted disturbance of all social conditions, eternal uncertainty and unrest - these distinguish the bourgeois period from all earlier ones. All fixed, frozen relations, with their associations of ancient and esteemed prejudices and opinions, are swept away; all newly formed ones become old-fashioned before they can fossilize. All that is solid melts into air, all that is holy is made unclean, and man is at last compelled to face with sober senses, his real conditions of life, and his relations with his kind.

The need of a constantly expanding market for its products chases the bourgeoisie over the whole surface of the globe. It must nestle everywhere, settle everywhere, establish connections everywhere.

The bourgeoisie has through its exploitation of the world market given a urban character to production and consumption in every country. To the great distress of Reactionists, it has drawn from under the feet of industry the national ground on which it stood. All old, established national industries have been destroyed or are daily being destroyed. They are pushed aside by new industries, whose introduction becomes a life-and-death question for all civilized nations, by industries that no longer work up local raw material, but raw material drawn from most faraway places; industries whose products are consumed, not only at home, but in every portion of the globe. In place of the old wants, satisfied by the productions of the country, we find new wants, requiring for their satisfaction the products of distant lands and climates. In place of the old local and national seclusion and self-sufficiency, we have interaction in every direction, universal interdependence of nations. And as in material, so also in intellectual production. The intellectual creations of individual nations become common property. National one-sidedness and narrow-mindedness become more and more impossible, and from the many national and local literatures, there comes a world literature.

The bourgeoisie, by the rapid improvement of all tools of production, by the methods of communication being made so much easier, brings all, even the most barbarian, nations into civilization. The cheap prices of its products are the heavy artillery it uses to batter down all Chinese walls, with which it forces their intense hatred of foreigners to give in. It requires all nations, on pain of of extinction, to adopt the bourgeois mode of production; it requires them to introduce what it calls civilization into their midst, i.e., to become bourgeois themselves. In short, it creates a world after its own image.

The bourgeoisie has put the country under the rule of the towns. It has created enormous cities, has greatly increased the urban population as compared with the rural, and has in this way rescued a considerable part of the population from the idiocy of rural life. Just as it has made the country dependent on the towns, so it has made barbarian and semi-barbarian countries dependent on the civilized ones, nations of peasants on nations of bourgeois, the East on the West.

The bourgeoisie keeps more and more elimination of the scattered state of the population, of the means of production, and of property. It has combined production, and has concentrated property in a few hands. The necessary consequence of this was political centralization. Independent, or but loosely connected provinces, with separate interests, laws, governments and systems of taxation, became lumped together into one nation, with one government, one code of laws, one national class-interest, one frontier and one customs tariff. The bourgeoisie, during its rule of barely one hundred years, has created more massive and more colossal productive forces than have all previous generations together. Subjection of Nature's forces to man, machinery, application of chemistry to industry and agriculture, steam navigation, railways, electric telegraphs, clearing of whole continents for cultivation, canalization of rivers, whole populations magically brought out of the ground -- what earlier century could even dream that such productive forces slept in the lap of social labour?

We see then: the means of production and of exchange, on whose foundation the bourgeoisie built itself up, were generated in feudal society. At a certain stage in the development of these means of production and of exchange, the conditions under which feudal society produced and exchanged, the feudal organization of agriculture and manufacturing industry, in short, the feudal relations of property became no longer compatible with the already developed productive forces; they became like chains. They had to be burst; they were burst.

Into their place stepped free competition, accompanied by a social and political constitution adapted to it, and by the economical and political sway of the bourgeois class.

A similar movement is going on before our own eyes. Modern bourgeois society with its relations of production, of exchange and of property, a society that has magically created such gigantic means of production and of exchange, is like the sorcerer who is no longer able to control the powers of the spirit world whom he has called up by his spells. For many a decade past the history of industry and commerce is only the history of the revolt of modern productive forces against modern conditions of production, against the property relations that are the conditions for the existence of the bourgeoisie and of its rule. It is enough to mention the commercial panics that by their periodical return put on its trial, each time more threateningly, the existence of the entire bourgeois society. In these crises a great part not only of the existing products, but also of the previously created productive forces, are periodically destroyed. In these crises there breaks out an epidemic that, in all earlier periods of time, would have seemed ridiculous -- the epidemic of overproduction. Society suddenly finds itself put back into a state of momentary barbarism; it appears as if a famine or a universal war of devastation had cut off the supply of every way to survive; industry and commerce seem to be destroyed; and why?

Because there is too much civilization, too many resources, too much industry, too much commerce. The productive forces at the disposal of society no longer tend to further the development of the conditions of bourgeois property; instead, they have become too powerful for these conditions, by which they are chained, and so soon as they overcome these fetters, they bring disorder into the whole of bourgeois society, endanger the existence of bourgeois property. The conditions of bourgeois society are too narrow to take in the wealth created by them. And how does the bourgeoisie get over these crises? On the one hand enforced destruction of a quantity of productive forces; on the other, by the conquest of new markets, and by the more thorough exploitation of the old ones. That is to say, by paving the way for even worse problems, and reducing the ability to prevent them.

The weapons with which the bourgeoisie toppled feudalism to the ground are now turned against the bourgeoisie itself.

But not only has the bourgeoisie forged the weapons that bring death to itself; it has also called into existence the men who are to wield those weapons -- the modern working class -- the proletarians.

In proportion as the bourgeoisie, i.e., capital, is developed, in the same proportion is the proletariat, the modern working class, developed -- a class of laborers, who live only as long as they find work, and who find work only so long as their labour increases capital. These laborers, who must sell themselves piece by piece, are a product, like every other item of commerce, and are because of this are exposed to all the ups and downs of competition, to all the unreliability of the market.

Owing to all the use of machinery and to division of labour, the work of the proletarians has lost all individual character, and consequently, all enjoyment for the workman. He becomes a limb of the machine, and it is only the most simple, most boring, and most easily acquired knack that is required of him. So the cost of production of a workman is restricted, almost entirely, to the subsistence that he requires for his maintenance, and for the propagation of his race. But the price of a commodity, and therefore also of labour, is equal to its cost of production. In proportion therefore, as the awfulness of the work increases, the wage decreases. In proportion as the use of machinery and division of labour increases, in the same proportion the burden of work also increases, whether by lengthening of the working hours, by increase of the work in a given time or by increased speed of the machinery, etc.

Modern industry has converted the little workshop of the fatherly master into the great factory of the industrial capitalist. Large groups of laborers, crowded into the factory, are organized like soldiers. As privates of the industrial army they are placed under the command of a perfect hierarchy of officers and sergeants. Not only are they slaves of the bourgeois class, and of the bourgeois State; they are every day and every hour enslaved by the machine, by the over-looker, and, above all, by the individual bourgeois manufacturer himself. The more openly this tyranny announces that personal gain to be its end and aim, the more petty, the more hateful and the more depressing it is.

The less the skill and use of strength is required in manual labour, in other words the more modern industry becomes developed, the more is the labour of men replaced by that of women. Differences of age and sex have no longer any distinctive social meaning for the working class. All are instruments of labour, more or less expensive to use, according to their age and sex.

No sooner is the exploitation of the laborer by the manufacturer so far at an end, that he receives his wages in cash, than he is taken advantage of by the other portions of the bourgeoisie: the landlord, the shopkeeper, the pawnbroker, etc.

The lower levels of the middle class -- the small tradespeople, shopkeepers, retired tradesmen generally, the handicraftsmen and peasants -- all these sink gradually into the proletariat, partly because their small amount of capital is not enough for the scale on which Modern Industry is carried on, and is swamped in the competition with the large capitalists, partly because their specialized skill is made worthless by the new methods of production. In this way the proletariat is recruited from all classes of the population.

The proletariat goes through various stages of development. With its birth begins its struggle with the bourgeoisie. At first the contest is carried on by individual laborers, then by the workpeople of a factory, then by the leaders of one trade, in one location, against the individual bourgeois who directly exploits them. They direct their attacks not against the bourgeois conditions of production, but against the tools of production themselves; they destroy imported goods that compete with their labour, they smash to pieces machinery, they set factories on fire, they try to restore by force the now-gone status of the workman of the Middle Ages.

At this stage the laborers still form an unorganized mass scattered over the whole country, and broken up by their mutual competition. If they unite anywhere to form more compact group, this is not yet the consequence of their own actions, but of the union of the bourgeoisie, which in order to achieve its own political ends must set the whole proletariat in motion, and is also still able to do so. At this stage, therefore, the proletarians do not fight their enemies, but the enemies of their enemies, what still remains of absolute monarchy, the landowners, the non-industrial bourgeois, the unimportant bourgeoisie. In this way the whole historical movement is concentrated in the hands of the bourgeoisie; every victory the proletariat gets is a victory for the bourgeoisie.

But with the development of industry the proletariat not only increases in number; it becomes more and more concentrated together, its strength grows, and it feels that strength more. The various interests and conditions of life within the ranks of the proletariat are made more and more equal, in proportion as machinery gets rid of all distinctions of labour, and nearly everywhere reduces wages to the same low level. The growing competition among the bourgeois, and the resulting commercial crises, make the wages of the workers even more unreliable. The constant improvement of machinery, always more rapidly developing, makes their livelihood more and more likely to become impossible; the collisions between individual workmen and individual bourgeois become more and more like collisions between two classes. So the workers begin to form combinations (Trades Unions) against the bourgeois; they join together in order to keep up the rate of wages; they establish permanent associations in order to prepare for occasional rebellions. Here and there the contest breaks out into riots.

Now and then the workers are victorious, but only for a time. The real result of their battles lies, not in the immediate result, but in the always-expanding union of the workers. This union is helped on by the improved ways of communication that are created by modern industry and that place the workers of different localities in contact with one another. It was just this contact that was needed to centralize the many local struggles, all of the same type, into one national struggle between classes. But every class struggle is a political struggle. And that union, to manage what the middle class of the Middle Ages, with their puny highways, required centuries, the modern proletarians, thanks to railways, achieve in a few years.

This organization of the proletarians into a class, and so into a political party, is always being upset again by the competition between the workers themselves. But it always rises up again, stronger, firmer, mightier. It forces legislative recognition of particular interests of the workers, by taking advantage of the divisions among the bourgeoisie itself. This is how the ten-hours' bill in England was carried.

The collisions between the classes of the old society further, in many ways, the course of development of the proletariat. The bourgeoisie finds itself involved in a constant battle. At first with the aristocracy; later on, with those portions of the bourgeoisie itself, whose interests have become opposed to the progress of industry; at all times, with the bourgeoisie of foreign countries. In all these battles it sees itself forced to become appealing to the proletariat, to ask for its help, and in this way, to drag it into the political arena. The bourgeoisie itself, therefore, provides the proletariat with weapons for fighting the bourgeoisie.

Further, as we have already seen, entire sections of the ruling classes are, by the advance of industry, brought into the proletariat, or are at least threatened in their conditions of existence. These also supply the proletariat with new elements of knowledge and progress.

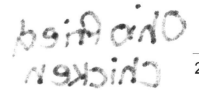

25

Finally, in times when the class struggle comes close to the most important time, the process of dissolving going on within the ruling class, in fact within the whole range of society, takes on such a violent, obvious character, that a small section of the ruling class cuts itself free, and joins the revolutionary class, the class that holds the future in its hands. Just as at an earlier period, a section of the nobility went over to the bourgeoisie, so now a portion of the bourgeoisie goes over to the proletariat, and in particular, a portion of the bourgeois intellectuals who have raised themselves to the level of understanding the historical movement as a whole.

Of all the classes that stand face to face with the bourgeoisie today, the proletariat alone is a really revolutionary class. The other classes decay and finally disappear in the face of Modern Industry; the proletariat is its special and essential product. The lower middle class, the small manufacturer, the shopkeeper, the artisan, the peasant, all these fight against the bourgeoisie, to save from extinction their existence as fractions of the middle class. They are therefore not revolutionary, but conservative. Actually they are reactionary, for they try to roll back the wheel of history. If by chance they are revolutionary, they are only that way because of their future transfer into the proletariat, defending not their present, but their future interests. They leave their own standpoint to place themselves at that of the proletariat.

The "dangerous class," the social scum, that rotting mass thrown off by the lowest layers of old society, may, here and there, be swept into the movement by a proletarian revolution; its conditions of life, however, make it more likely to be easily bribed by the reactionaries.

In the conditions of the proletariat, those of old society at large are already virtually swamped. The proletarian has no property; his relationships with his wife and children has no longer anything in common with the bourgeois family-relations; modern industrial labour, modern subjection to capital, the same in England as in France, in America as in Germany, has taken away from him every hint of national character. Law, morality, religion, these are to him just bourgeois prejudices, behind which wait in ambush just as many bourgeois interests.

All the previous classes that got the advantage tried to strengthen their already acquired status by subjecting society at in general to their conditions. The proletarians cannot become masters of the productive forces of society except by getting rid of their own former ways of getting things, and thereby also every other ways of getting things. They have nothing of their own to strengthen and keep safe; their mission is to destroy the concept of individual property.

All previous historical movements were movements of minorities, or in the interests of minorities. The proletarian movement is the self-conscious, independent movement of the immense majority, in the interests of the immense majority. The proletariat, the lowest level of our current society, cannot stir, cannot raise itself up, without all the other layers of official society crumbling.

The struggle of the proletariat with the bourgeoisie is at first a national struggle. The proletariat of each country must, of course, first of all settle matters with its own bourgeoisie.

In depicting the most general phases of the development of the proletariat, we traced the more or less disguised civil war, raging within existing society, up to the point where that war breaks out into open revolution, and where the violent overthrow of the bourgeoisie lays the foundation for the rule of the proletariat.

Up until now every form of society has been based, as we have already seen, on the fighting between oppressing and oppressed classes. But in order to oppress a class, certain conditions must be assured to it under which it can, at least, continue its slave-like existence. The serf, in the period of serfdom, raised himself to membership in the commune, just as the petty bourgeois, in the chains of feudal absolutism, managed to develop into a real bourgeois. The modern laborer, though, instead of rising with the progress of industry, sinks deeper and deeper below the conditions of existence of his own class. He becomes desperately poor, and poverty develops more rapidly than population and wealth. And here it becomes obvious that the bourgeoisie is no longer capable of being the ruling class in society, and to force its conditions of existence upon society as an overriding law. It is unfit to rule because it is unable to promise an existence to its slave within his slavery, because it cannot help letting him sink into such a situation that it has to feed him, instead of being fed by him. Society can no longer live under this bourgeoisie, in other words, its existence is no longer compatible with society.

The essential condition for the existence, and for the rule of the bourgeois class, is the creation and increasing of capital; the condition for capital is wage-labour. Wage-labour depends entirely on competition between the laborers. The advance of industry, whose helpless promoter is the bourgeoisie, replaces the isolation of the laborers, due to competition, by their revolutionary combination, due to association. The development of Modern Industry, therefore, cuts from under its feet the very foundation on which the bourgeoisie produces and appropriates products. What the bourgeoisie, therefore, produces, above all, is its own grave-diggers. Its fall and the victory of the proletariat are equally inevitable.

II. Proletarians and Communists

In what relation do the Communists stand to the proletarians as a whole?

The Communists do not form a separate party against to other working-class parties.

They have no interests separate and apart from those of the proletariat as a whole.

They do not set up any group-based principles of their own, by which to shape and mold the proletarian movement.

The Communists are distinguished from the other working-class parties by only these things: (1) In the national struggles of the proletarians of the different countries, they point out and bring to the front the shared interests of entire proletariat, not related to nationality. (2) In the various stages of development which the struggle of the working class against the bourgeoisie has to pass through, they always and everywhere represent the interests of the movement as a whole.

The Communists, therefore, are on the one hand, practically, the most advanced and resolute section of the working-class parties of every country, that section which pushes forward all others; on the other hand, theoretically, they have over the great mass of the proletariat the advantage of clearly understanding the situation.

The immediate goal of the Communism is the same as that of all the other proletarian parties: formation of the proletariat into a class, overthrow of the bourgeois rule, conquest of political power by the proletariat.

The theoretical conclusions of the Communists are in no way based on ideas or principles that have been invented, or discovered, by this or that would-be universal reformer. They simply express, in general terms, actual relationships springing from an existing class struggle, from a historical movement going on under our very eyes. Getting rid of existing property concepts is not at all a distinctive feature of Communism.

All property relations in the past have always been changed as a result of change in historical conditions.

The French Revolution, for example, got rid of feudal property in favor of bourgeois property.

The distinguishing feature of Communism is not the getting rid of property in general, but the getting rid of bourgeois property. But modern bourgeois private property is the final and most complete expression of the system of producing and deciding ownership products; that is based on the exploitation of the many by the few.

In this sense, the theory of the Communists may be summed up in the single sentence: Abolition of private property.

We Communists have been criticized wanting to abolish the right of personally acquiring property as the fruit of a man's own labour, which property is said to be the groundwork of all personal freedom, activity and independence.

Hard-won, self-acquired, self-earned property! Do you mean the property of the minor artisan and of the small peasant, a form of property that came before the bourgeois form? There is no need to abolish that; the development of industry has mostly already destroyed it, and is still destroying it daily.

Or do you mean modern bourgeois private property?

But does wage-labour create any property for the laborer? Not a bit. It creates capital, i.e. that kind of property which exploits wage-labour, and which cannot increase except by creating a new supply of wage-labour for fresh exploitation. Property, in its current form, is based on capital and wage-labour being enemies. Let us examine both sides of this antagonism.

To be a capitalist is to have not only a purely personal, but also a social status in production. Capital is a collective product, and only by the united action of many members can it be set in motion.

Capital is, therefore, not a personal, it is a social power.

When, therefore, capital is converted into common property, into the property of all members of society, personal property is not thereby transformed into social property. It is only the social character of the property that is changed. It loses its class-character.

Let us now take wage-labour.

The average price of wage-labour is the minimum wage, i.e., the means of subsistence, which is absolutely required in bare existence as a laborer. What, therefore, the wage-laborer manages to get through his labour is just enough to keep going and reproduce a bare existence. We by no means intend to abolish this personal appropriation of the products of labour, an appropriation that is made for the maintenance and reproduction of human life, and that leaves no surplus wherewith to command the labour of others. All that we want to do away with is the miserable nature of this appropriation, under which the laborer lives just to increase capital, and is allowed to live only in so far as the interest of the ruling class requires it.

In bourgeois society, living labour is nothing but a way to increase accumulated labour. In Communist society, accumulated labour is a way to widen, to enrich, to promote the existence of the laborer.

In bourgeois society, therefore, the past dominates the present; in Communist society, the present dominates the past. In bourgeois society capital is independent and has individuality, while the living person is dependent and has no individuality.

And the abolition of this state of things is called by the bourgeois, abolition of individuality and freedom! And rightly so. The abolition of bourgeois individuality, bourgeois independence, and bourgeois freedom is undoubtedly aimed for.

By freedom is meant, under the present bourgeois conditions of production, free trade, free selling and buying. But if selling and buying disappears, free selling and buying disappears also. This talk about free selling and buying, and all the other "brave words" of our bourgeoisie about freedom in general, have a meaning, if any, only in contrast with restricted selling and buying, with the restricted traders of the Middle Ages, but have no meaning when opposed to the Communistic abolition of buying and selling, of the bourgeois conditions of production, and of the bourgeoisie itself.

You are horrified at our intending get rid of private property. But in your existing society, private property is already done away with for nine-tenths of the population; its existence for the few is solely due to its non-existence in the hands of those nine-tenths. You criticize us, therefore, with intending to do away with a form of property, the necessary condition for whose existence is the non-existence of any property for the immense majority of society.

Simply put, you reproach us with intending to do away with your property. Yes, that is just what we intend.

From the moment when labour can no longer be converted into capital, money, or rent, into a social power capable of being monopolized, i.e., from the moment when individual property can no longer be transformed into bourgeois property, into capital, from that moment, you say individuality vanishes.

You must, therefore, confess that by "individual" you mean no other person than the bourgeois, than the middle-class owner of property. This person must, indeed, be swept out of the way, and made impossible.

Communism deprives no man of the power to appropriate the products of society; all that it does is to deprive him of the power to subjugate the labour of others by means of such appropriation.

It has been objected that upon the abolition of private property all work will cease, and universal laziness will overtake us.

According to this, bourgeois society should long ago have been destroyed through idleness; for those of its members who work, acquire nothing, and those who acquire anything, do not work. The whole of this objection is just another expression of the obvious statement: that there can no longer be any wage-labour when there is no longer any capital.

All objections urged against the Communistic mode of producing and appropriating material products, have, in the same way, been urged against the Communistic modes of producing and appropriating intellectual products. Just as, to the bourgeois, the disappearance of class property is the disappearance of production itself, so the disappearance of class culture is to him identical with the disappearance of all culture.

That culture, the loss of which he laments, is, for the enormous majority, a mere training to act as a machine.

But don't wrangle with us so long as you apply, to our intended abolition of bourgeois property, the standard of your bourgeois notions of freedom, culture, law, etc. Your very ideas are just the outgrowth of the conditions of your bourgeois production and bourgeois property, just as your wisdom is but the will of your class made into a law for all, a will, whose essential character and direction are determined by the economical conditions of existence of your class.

The selfish misconception that induces you to transform into eternal laws of nature and of reason, the social forms springing from your present mode of production and form of property-historical relations that rise and disappear in the progress of production -- this misconception you share with every ruling class that has preceded you. What you see clearly in the case of ancient property, what you admit in the case of feudal property, you are of course forbidden to admit in the case of your own bourgeois form of property.

Abolition of the family! Even the most radical flare up at this infamous proposal of the Communists.

On what foundation is the present family, the bourgeois family, based? On capital, on private gain. In its completely developed form this family exists only among the bourgeoisie. But this state of things finds its complement in the practical absence of the family among the proletarians, and in public prostitution.

The bourgeois family will vanish as a matter of course when its complement vanishes, and both will vanish with the vanishing of capital.

Do you charge us with wanting to stop the exploitation of children by their parents? To this crime we plead guilty.

But, you will say, we destroy the most sacred of relations, when we replace home education by social.

And your education! Is not that also social, and determined by the social conditions under which you educate, by the intervention, direct or indirect, of society, by means of schools, etc.? The Communists have not invented the intervention of society in education; they only want to change the character of that intervention, and to rescue education from the influence of the ruling class.

The bourgeois clap-trap about the family and education, about the hallowed co-relation of parent and child, becomes all the more disgusting, the more, by the action of Modern Industry, all family ties among the proletarians are torn asunder, and their children transformed into simple articles of commerce and instruments of labour.

But you Communists would introduce community of women, screams the whole bourgeoisie in chorus.

The bourgeois sees in his wife a mere instrument of production. He hears that the instruments of production are to be exploited in common, and, naturally, can come to no other conclusion than that the lot of being common to all will likewise fall to the women.

He has not even a suspicion that the real point is to do away with the status of women as mere instruments of production.

For the rest, nothing is more ridiculous than the virtuous indignation of our bourgeois at the community of women which, they pretend, is to be openly and officially established by the Communists. The Communists have no need to introduce community of women; it has existed almost from time immemorial.

Our bourgeois, not thinking it enough to have wives and daughters of their proletarians to do with what they like, not even mentioning common prostitutes, take the greatest pleasure in seducing each other's wives.

Bourgeois marriage is in reality a system of shared wives and also, at the most, what the Communists might possibly be reproached with, is that they desire to introduce,in substitution for a hypocritically concealed, an openly legalized community of women. For the rest, it is self-evident that the abolition of the present system of production must bring with it the abolition of the community of women springing from that system, i.e., of prostitution both public and private.

The Communists are further reproached with desiring to abolish countries and nationality.

The working men have no country. We cannot take from them what they have not got. Since the proletariat must first of all acquire political supremacy, must rise to be the leading class of the nation, must constitute itself the nation, it is, so far, itself national, though not in the bourgeois sense of the word.

National differences and antagonisms between peoples are daily more and more vanishing, owing to the development of the bourgeoisie, to freedom of commerce, to the world-market, to uniformity in the mode of production and in the conditions of life corresponding thereto.

The supremacy of the proletariat will cause them to vanish even faster. United action, of the leading civilized countries at least, is one of the first conditions for the emancipation of the proletariat.

In proportion as the exploitation of one individual by another is put an end to, the exploitation of one nation by another will also be put an end to. In proportion as the antagonism between classes within the nation vanishes, the hostility of one nation to another will come to an end.

The charges against Communism made from a religious, a philosophical, and, generally, from an ideological standpoint, are not deserving of serious examination.

Does it require deep understanding to comprehend that man's ideas, views and conceptions, in one word, man's consciousness, changes with every change in the conditions of his material existence, in his social relations and in his social life?

What else does the history of ideas prove, than that intellectual production changes its nature as material production is changed? The ruling ideas of each age have always been the ideas of its ruling class.

When people speak of ideas that revolutionize society, they only express the fact that within the old society, the elements of a new one have been created, and that the dissolving of the old ideas keeps even pace with the dissolution of the old conditions of existence.

When the ancient world was in its last throes, the ancient religions were overcome by Christianity. When Christian ideas lost in the 18th century to rationalist ideas, feudal society fought its death battle with the then revolutionary bourgeoisie. The ideas of religious liberty and freedom of conscience merely gave expression to the sway of free competition within the domain of knowledge.

"Undoubtedly," it will be said, "religious, moral, philosophical and juridical ideas have been modified in the course of historical development. But religion, morality philosophy, political science, and law, constantly survived this change."

"There are, besides, eternal truths, such as Freedom, Justice, etc. that are common to all states of society. But Communism abolishes eternal truths, it abolishes all religion, and all morality, instead of constituting them on a new basis; it therefore acts in contradiction to all past historical experience."

What does this accusation reduce itself to? The history of all past society has consisted in the development of class antagonisms, antagonisms that assumed different forms at different epochs.

But whatever form they may have taken, one fact is common to all past ages: the exploitation of one part of society by the other. No wonder, then, that the social consciousness of past ages, despite all the multiplicity and variety it displays, moves within certain common forms, or general ideas, which cannot completely vanish except with the total disappearance of class antagonisms.

The Communist revolution is the most radical rupture with traditional property relations; no wonder that its development involves the most radical rupture with traditional ideas.

But enough with the bourgeois objections to Communism.

We have seen above, that the first step in the revolution by the working class, is to raise the proletariat to the position of ruling as to win the battle of democracy.

The proletariat will use its political supremacy to take control, by degrees, of all capital from the bourgeoisie, to centralize all instruments of production in the hands of the State, i.e., of the proletariat organized as the ruling class; and to increase the total of productive forces as rapidly as possible.

Of course, in the beginning, this cannot be done except by cruel attacks on the rights of property, and on the conditions of bourgeois production; by means of measures, therefore, which appear economically insufficient and unreliable, but which, in the course of the movement, go beyond themselves, cause the necessity of further inroads upon the old social order, and are unavoidable as a way to entirely revolutionize the mode of production.

These measures will of course be different in different countries.

Nevertheless in the most advanced countries, the following will be pretty generally applicable.

1. Abolition of property in land and application of all rents of land to public purposes.

2. A heavy progressive or graduated income tax.

3. Abolition of all right of inheritance.

4. Confiscation of the property of all emigrants and rebels.

5. Centralization of credit in the hands of the State, by means of a national bank with State capital and an exclusive monopoly.

6. Centralization of the means of communication and transport in the hands of the State.

7. Extension of factories and instruments of production owned by the State; the bringing into cultivation of wastelands, and the improvement of the soil generally in accordance with a common plan.

8. Equal liability of all to labour. Establishment of industrial armies, especially for agriculture.

9. Combination of agriculture with manufacturing industries; gradual abolition of the distinction between town and country, by a more equal distribution of the population over the country.

10. Free education for all children in public schools. Abolition of children's factory labour in its present form. Combination of education with industrial production, etc, etc.

When, in the course of development, class distinctions have disappeared, and all production has been concentrated in the hands of a vast association of the whole nation, the public power will lose its political character. Political power, properly so called, is just the organize power of one class for oppressing another. If the proletariat during its contest with the bourgeoisie is compelled, by the force of circumstances, to organize itself as a class, if, by means of a revolution, it makes itself the ruling class, and, as such, sweeps away by force the old conditions of production, then it will, along with these conditions, have swept away the conditions for the existence of class antagonisms and of classes generally, and will in this manner have abolished its own supremacy as a class.

In place of the old bourgeois society, with its classes and class antagonisms, we shall have an association, in which the free development of each is the condition for the free development of all.

III. Socialist and Communist Literature

1. REACTIONARY SOCIALISM

A. Feudal Socialism

Owing to their historical position, it became the chosen work of the aristocracies of France and England to write pamphlets against modern bourgeois society. In the French revolution of July 1830, and in the English reform agitation, these aristocracies again lost to the hateful enemy. From then on, a serious political contest was completely altogether out of the question. Only a literary battle remained possible. But even in the domain of literature the old cries of the restoration period had become impossible.

In order to arouse sympathy, the aristocracy had to lose sight, apparently, of their own interests, and to formulate their indictment against the bourgeoisie in the interest of the exploited working class alone. In this way the aristocracy took their revenge by singing mocking songs on their new master, and whispering in his ears sinister predictions of coming catastrophe.

In this way came about Feudal Socialism: half complaint, half comedy; half echo of the past, half menace of the future; at times, by its bitter, witty and incisive criticism, striking the bourgeoisie to the very heart's core; but always ridiculous in its effect, through total inability to comprehend the march of modern history.

The aristocracy, in order to rally the people to them, waved the proletarian alms-bag in front for a banner. But the people, as often as it joined them, saw on their buttocks the old feudal coats of arms, and deserted with loud and irreverent laughter.

One section of the French Legitimists and "Young England" were part of this spectacle.

In pointing out that their mode of exploitation was different to that of the bourgeoisie, the feudalists forget that they exploited under circumstances and conditions that were quite different, and that are now outdated. In showing that, under their rule, the modern proletariat never existed, they forget that the modern bourgeoisie is the necessary offspring of their own form of society.

For the rest, they do so little concealing the reactionary character of their criticism that their chief accusation against the bourgeoisie amounts to this: that under the bourgeois regime a class is being developed, which is destined to cut up root and branch the old order of society.

What they criticize the bourgeoisie with is not so much that it creates a proletariat, as that it creates a revolutionary proletariat.

In political practice, therefore, they join in all controlling measures against the working class; and in ordinary life, despite their fancy talk, they stoop to pick up the golden apples dropped from the tree of industry, and to trade truth, love, and honor for wool, sugar, and vodka.

As the parson has always gone hand in hand with the landlord, so has Clerical Socialism with Feudal Socialism.

Nothing is easier than to give Christian asceticism a Socialist tinge. Has not Christianity preached against private property, against marriage, against the State? Has it not preached in the place of these, charity and poverty, abstinence and ignoring the body, monastic life and Mother Church? Christian Socialism is simply the holy water with which the priest soothes the heart-burnings of the aristocrat.

B. Petty-Bourgeois Socialism

The feudal aristocracy was not the only class that has ruined by the bourgeoisie, not the only class whose conditions of existence pined and perished in the atmosphere of modern bourgeois society. The mediaeval burgesses and the small peasant proprietors were the ancestors of the modern bourgeoisie. In those countries which are but little developed, industrially and commercially, these two classes still exist side by side with the rising bourgeoisie.

In countries where modern civilization has become fully developed, a new class of petty bourgeois has been formed, moving between proletariat and bourgeoisie and always renewing itself as a part of bourgeois society. The individual members of this class, however, are being constantly hurled down into the proletariat by the action of competition, and, as modern industry develops, they even see the moment approaching when they will completely disappear as an independent section of modern society, to be replaced, in manufactures, agriculture and commerce, by overlookers, bailiffs and shopmen.

In countries like France, where the peasants make up far more than half of the population, it was natural that writers who sided with the proletariat against the bourgeoisie, should use, in their criticism of the bourgeois regime, the flag of the peasant and petty bourgeois, and from the standpoint of these intermediate classes should take up the cudgels for the working class. In this way came about petty-bourgeois Socialism. Sismondi was the leader of this school, not only in France but also in England.

This school of Socialism neatly picked apart the contradictions in the conditions of modern production. It laid bare the hypocritical excuses of economists. It proved, without question, the disastrous effects of machinery and division of labour; the concentration of capital and land in a few hands; overproduction and crises; it pointed out the inevitable ruin of the petty bourgeois and peasant, the misery of the proletariat, the anarchy in production, the crying inequalities in the distribution of wealth, the industrial war of extermination between nations, the dissolution of old moral bonds, of the old family relations, of the old nationalities.

In its positive goals, however, this form of Socialism plans either to restore the old means of production and of exchange, and with them the old property relations, and the old society, or to cramp the modern means of production and of exchange, within the framework of the old property relations that have been, and were bound to be, exploded by those means. In either case, it is both reactionary and Utopian.

Its last words are: corporate guilds for manufacture, patriarchal relations in agriculture.

Sorry, it's an impossible dream.

C. German, or "True," Socialism

The Socialist and Communist literature of France, a literature that originated under the pressure of a bourgeoisie in power, and that was the expression of the struggle against this power, was introduced into Germany at a time when the bourgeoisie, in that country, had just begun its contest with feudal absolutism.

German philosophers, would-be philosophers, and beaux esprits, eagerly seized on this literature, only forgetting, that when these writings immigrated from France into Germany, French social conditions had not immigrated along with them. In contact with German social conditions, this French literature lost all its immediate practical significance, and assumed a purely literary aspect. Thus, to the German philosophers of the eighteenth century, the demands of the first French Revolution were nothing more than the demands of "Practical Reason" in general, and the sayings of the wants of the revolutionary French bourgeoisie signified in their eyes the law of pure Will, of Will as it was going to be, of true human Will generally.

The world of the German literate consisted only in bringing the new French ideas into harmony with their ancient philosophical conscience, or rather, in copying the French ideas without deserting their own philosophic point of view.

This copying took place in the same way in which a foreign language is appropriated, namely, by translation.

It is well known how the monks wrote silly lives of Catholic Saints over the manuscripts on which the classical works of ancient religions had been written. The German literate reversed this process with the French literature. They wrote their philosophical nonsense beneath the French original. For instance, beneath the French criticism of the economic functions of money, they wrote "Alienation of Humanity," and beneath the French criticism of the bourgeois State they wrote "dethronement of the Category of the General," and so forth.

The introduction of these philosophical phrases at the back of the French historical criticisms they dubbed "Philosophy of Action," "True Socialism," "German Science of Socialism," "Philosophical Foundation of Socialism," and so on.

The French Socialist and Communist literature was thus made completely useless. And, since it stopped in the hands of the German to express the struggle of one class with the other, he felt conscious of having overcome "French one-sidedness" and of representing, not true requirements, but the requirements of truth; not the interests of the proletariat, but the interests of Human Nature, of Man in general, who belongs to no class, has no reality, who exists only in the misty realm of philosophical fantasy.

This German Socialism, which took its schoolboy task so seriously and solemnly, and praised its poor stock-in-trade in such silly fashion, meanwhile gradually lost its childish innocence.

The fight of the German, and especially, of the Prussian bourgeoisie, against feudal aristocracy and absolute monarchy, in other words, the liberal movement, became more earnest.

By this, the long wished-for opportunity was offered to "True" Socialism of confronting the political movement with the Socialist demands, of hurling the traditional forbiddings against liberalism, against representative government, against bourgeois competition, bourgeois freedom of the press, bourgeois legislation, bourgeois liberty and equality, and of preaching to the masses that they had nothing to gain, and everything to lose, by this bourgeois movement. German Socialism forgot, in the nick of time, that the French criticism, whose silly echo it was, assumed beforehand the existence of modern bourgeois society, with its corresponding economic conditions of existence, and the political constitution adapted thereto, the very things whose attainment was the object of the pending struggle in Germany.

To the absolute governments, with their following of parsons, professors, country squires and officials, it served as a welcome scarecrow against the threatening bourgeoisie.

It was a sweet finish after the bitter pills of floggings and bullets with which these same governments, just at that time, dosed the German working-class risings.

While this "True" Socialism thus served the governments as a weapon for fighting the German bourgeoisie, it, at the same time, directly represented a reactionary interest, the interest of the German Philistines. In Germany the petty-bourgeois class, a relic of the sixteenth century, and since then constantly cropping up again under various forms, is the real social basis of the existing state of things.

To preserve this class is to preserve the existing state of things in Germany. The industrial and political supremacy of the bourgeoisie threatens it with certain destruction; on the one hand, from the concentration of capital; on the other, from the rise of a revolutionary proletariat. "True" Socialism appeared to kill these two birds with one stone. It spread like an epidemic.

The robe of speculative cobwebs, embroidered with flowers of rhetoric, steeped in the dew of sickly sentiment, this transcendental robe in which the German Socialists wrapped their sorry "eternal truths," all skin and bone, served to wonderfully increase the sale of their goods amongst such a public.

And on its part, German Socialism recognized, more and more, its own calling as the loud and annoying representative of the petty- bourgeois Philistine.

It proclaimed the German nation to be the model nation, and the German petty Philistine to be the typical man. To every bad quality of this model man it gave a hidden, higher, Socialistic interpretation, the exact opposite of its real character. It went to the extreme length of directly opposing the "brutally destructive" tendency of Communism, and of proclaiming its supreme and impartial contempt of all class struggles. With very few exceptions, all the so-called Socialist and Communist publications that now (1847) circulate in Germany belong to the domain of this foul and enervating literature.

2. CONSERVATIVE, OR BOURGEOIS, SOCIALISM

A part of the bourgeoisie wants to make up for social grievances, in order to secure the continued existence of bourgeois society.

To this section belong economists, philanthropists, humanitarians, improvers of the condition of the working class, organisers of charity, members of societies for the prevention of cruelty to animals, temperance fanatics, hole-and-corner reformers of every imaginable kind. This form of Socialism has, moreover, been worked out into complete systems.

We may site Proudhon's Philosophie de la Misere as an example of this form.

The Socialistic bourgeois want all the advantages of modern social conditions without the struggles and dangers necessarily resulting from it. They desire the existing state of society minus its revolutionary and disintegrating elements. They wish for a bourgeoisie without a proletariat. The bourgeoisie naturally conceives the world in which it is supreme to be the best; and bourgeois Socialism develops this comfortable conception into various more or less complete systems. In requiring the proletariat to carry out such a system, and thereby to march straightway into the social New Jerusalem, it but requires in reality, that the proletariat should remain within the bounds of existing society, but should cast away all its hateful ideas concerning the bourgeoisie.

A second and more practical, but less systematic, form of this Socialism sought to reduce every revolutionary movement in the eyes of the working class, by showing that no mere political reform, but only a change in the material conditions of existence, in economic relations, could be of any advantage to them. By changes in the material conditions of existence, this form of Socialism, however, by no means understands abolition of the bourgeois relations of production, an abolition that can be effected only by a revolution, but administrative reforms, based on the continued existence of these relations; reforms, therefore, that in no respect affect the relations between capital and labour, but, at the best, lessen the cost, and simplify the administrative work, of bourgeois government.

Bourgeois Socialism reaches adequate expression, when, and only when, it becomes a mere figure of speech.

Free trade: for the benefit of the working class. Protective duties: for the benefit of the working class. Prison Reform: for the benefit of the working class. This is the last word and the only seriously meant word of bourgeois Socialism.

It is summed up in the phrase: the bourgeois is a bourgeois -- for the benefit of the working class.

3. CRITICAL-UTOPIAN SOCIALISM AND COMMUNISM

We do not here refer to that literature which, in every great modern revolution, has always given voice to the demands of the proletariat, such as the writings of Babeuf and others.

The first direct attempts of the proletariat to attain its own ends, made in times of universal excitement, when feudal society was being overthrown, these attempts necessarily failed, owing to the then undeveloped state of the proletariat, as well as to the absence of the economic conditions for its emancipation, conditions that had yet to be produced, and could be produced by the impending bourgeois epoch alone. The revolutionary literature that accompanied these first movements of the proletariat had necessarily a reactionary character. It inculcated universal asceticism and social levelling in its crudest form.

The Socialist and Communist systems properly so called, those of Saint-Simon, Fourier, Owen and others, spring into existence in the early undeveloped period, described above, of the struggle between proletariat and bourgeoisie (see Section 1. Bourgeois and Proletarians).

The founders of these systems see, indeed, the class antagonisms, as well as the action of the decomposing elements, in the prevailing form of society. But the proletariat, as yet in its infancy, offers to them the spectacle of a class without any historical initiative or any independent political movement.

Since the development of class antagonism keeps even pace with the development of industry, the economic situation, as they find it, does not as yet offer to them the material conditions for the emancipation of the proletariat. They therefore search after a new social science, after new social laws, that are to create these conditions.

Historical action is to yield to their personal inventive action, historically created conditions of emancipation to fantastic ones, and the gradual, spontaneous class-organization of the proletariat to the organization of society specially contrived by these inventors. Future history resolves itself, in their eyes, into the propaganda and the practical carrying out of their social plans.

In the formation of their plans they are conscious of caring chiefly for the interests of the working class, as being the most suffering class. Only from the point of view of being the most suffering class does the proletariat exist for them.

The undeveloped state of the class struggle, as well as their own surroundings, causes Socialists of this kind to consider themselves far better than all class antagonisms. They want to improve the condition of every member of society, even that of the most favored. So they frequently appeal to society at large, without distinction of class; nay, by preference, to the ruling class. For how can people, when once they understand their system, fail to see in it the best possible plan of the best possible state of society?

So they reject all political, and especially all revolutionary, action; they wish to achieve their ends by peaceful means, and endeavor, by small experiments, necessarily doomed to failure, and by the force of example, to pave the way for the new social Gospel.

Such unbelievable pictures of future society, painted at a time when the proletariat is still in a very undeveloped state and has only a very unrealistic conception of its own position correspond with the first instinctive yearnings of that class for a general reconstruction of society.

But these Socialist and Communist publications contain also a critical element. They attack every principle of existing society. Hence they are full of the most valuable materials for the enlightenment of the working class. The practical measures proposed in them -- such as the abolition of the distinction between town and country, of the family, of the carrying on of industries for the account of private individuals, and of the wage system, the proclamation of social harmony, the conversion of the functions of the State into just an organization of production, all these proposals, point solely to the disappearance of class antagonisms which were, at that time, only just cropping up, and which, in these publications, are recognized in their earliest, indistinct and undefined forms only. These proposals, therefore, are of a purely Utopian character.

The significance of Critical-Utopian Socialism and Communism bears an inverse relation to historical development. In proportion as the modern class struggle develops and takes definite shape, this fantastic standing apart from the contest, these fantastic attacks on it, lose all practical value and all theoretical justification. Therefore, although the originators of these systems were, in many respects, revolutionary, their disciples have, in every case, formed mere reactionary sects. They hold tight to the original views of their masters, in opposition to the progressive historical development of the proletariat. They, therefore, endeavor, and that consistently, to deaden the class struggle and to reconcile the class antagonisms. They still dream of experimental realization of their social Utopias, of founding isolated "phalansteres," of establishing "Home Colonies," of setting up a "Little Icaria" -- duodecimo editions of the New Jerusalem -- and to realize all these castles in the air, they are compelled to appeal to the feelings and purses of the bourgeois. By degrees they sink into the category of the reactionary conservative Socialists depicted above, differing from these only by more systematic pedantry, and by their fanatical and superstitious belief in the miraculous effects of their social science.

They, therefore, violently oppose all political action on the part of the working class; such action, according to them, can only result from blind unbelief in the new Gospel.

The Owenites in England, and the Fourierists in France, respectively, oppose the Chartists and the Reformistes.

IV. Positions of the Communists in Relation to the Various Existing Opposition Parties

Section II has made clear the relations of the Communists to the existing working-class parties, such as the Chartists in England and the Agrarian Reformers in America.

The Communists fight for the attainment of the immediate aims, for the enforcement of the momentary interests of the working class; but in the movement of the present, they also represent and take care of the future of that movement. In France the Communists ally themselves with the Social-Democrats, against the conservative and radical bourgeoisie, reserving, however, the right to take up a critical position in regard to phrases and illusions traditionally handed down from the great Revolution.

In Switzerland they support the Radicals, without losing sight of the fact that this party consists of antagonistic elements, partly of Democratic Socialists, in the French sense, partly of radical bourgeois.

In Poland they support the party that insists on an agrarian revolution as the prime condition for national emancipation, that party which fomented the insurrection of Cracow in 1846.

In Germany they fight with the bourgeoisie whenever it acts in a revolutionary way, against the absolute monarchy, the feudal squirearchy, and the petty bourgeoisie.

But they never cease, for a single instant, to establish into the minds of the working class the clearest possible recognition of the hostile antagonism between bourgeoisie and proletariat, in order that the German workers may straightaway use, as so many weapons against the bourgeoisie, the social and political conditions that the bourgeoisie must necessarily introduce along with its supremacy, and in order that, after the fall of the reactionary classes in Germany, the fight against the bourgeoisie itself may immediately begin.

The Communists turn their attention chiefly to Germany, because that country is on the eve of a bourgeois revolution that is bound to be carried out under more advanced conditions of European civilization, and with a much more developed proletariat, than that of England was in the seventeenth, and of France in the eighteenth century, and because the bourgeois revolution in Germany will be only the beginning of an immediately following proletarian revolution.

In short, the Communists everywhere support every revolutionary movement against the existing social and political order of things.

In all these movements they bring to the front, as the leading question in each, the property question, no matter what its degree of development at the time.

Finally, they work everywhere for the union and agreement of the democratic parties of all countries.

The Communists don't want to hide their views and aims. They openly declare that their ends can be attained only by the forcible overthrow of all existing social conditions. Let the ruling classes tremble at a Communistic revolution. The proletarians have nothing to lose but their chains. They have a world to win.

WORKING MEN OF ALL COUNTRIES, UNITE!

18546967R00040

Printed in Poland
by Amazon Fulfillment
Poland Sp. z o.o., Wrocław